COLORING BOOKS
FOR GROWN-UPS

Christmas Cards & Gift Tags

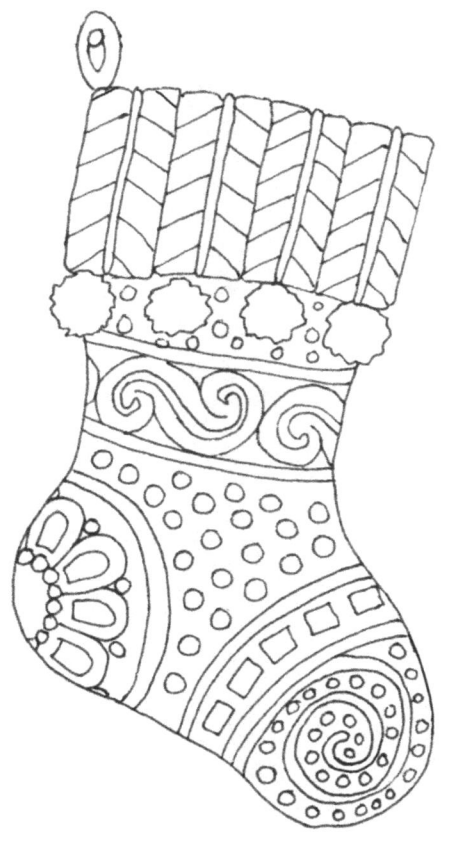

Illustrations and book design by Cheryl Casey.
© 2015 Cheryl Casey. All rights reserved.
ISBN-13: 978-1518684364
ISBN-10: 151868436X

cherylcaseyart.com

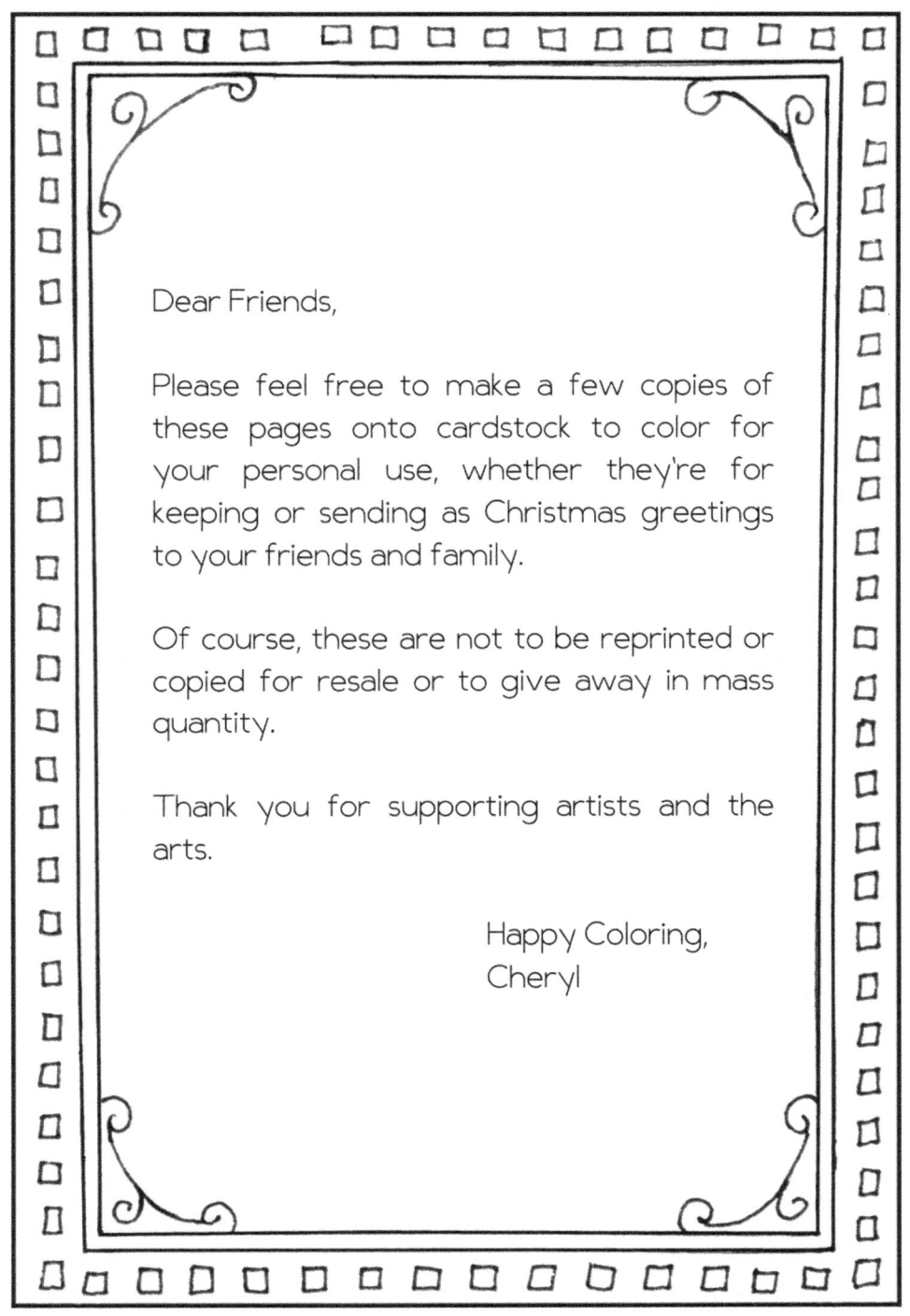

Dear Friends,

Please feel free to make a few copies of these pages onto cardstock to color for your personal use, whether they're for keeping or sending as Christmas greetings to your friends and family.

Of course, these are not to be reprinted or copied for resale or to give away in mass quantity.

Thank you for supporting artists and the arts.

Happy Coloring,
Cheryl

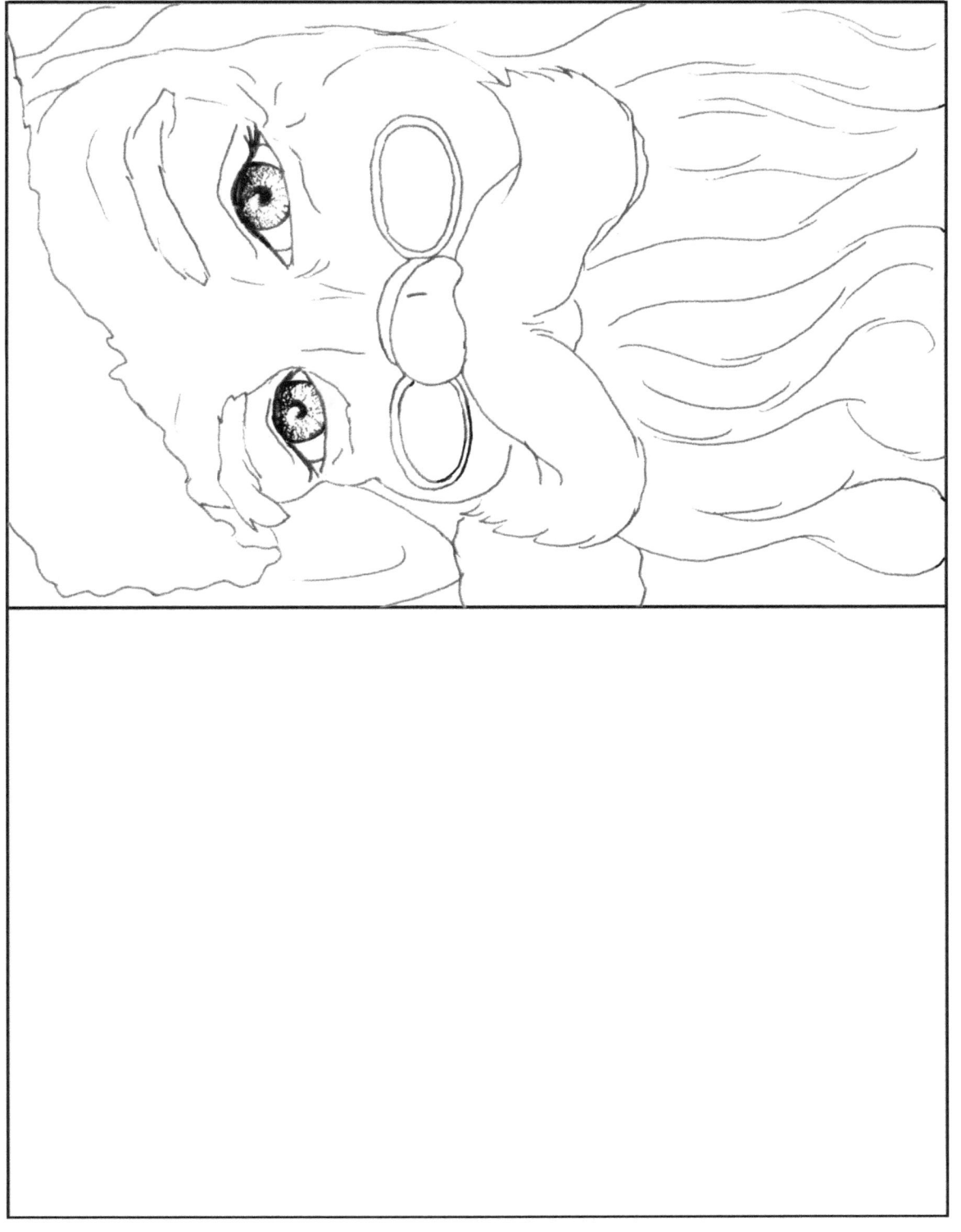

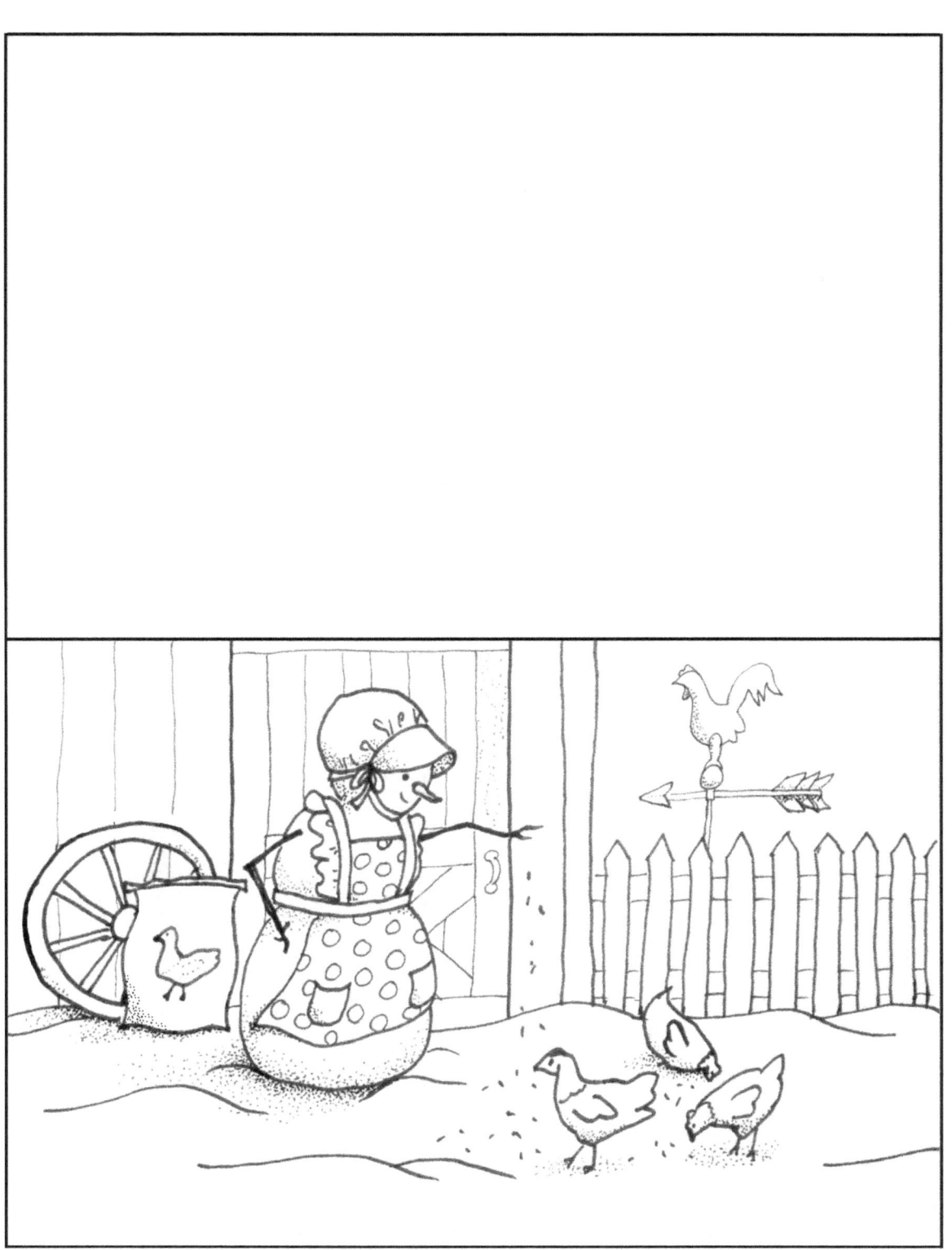

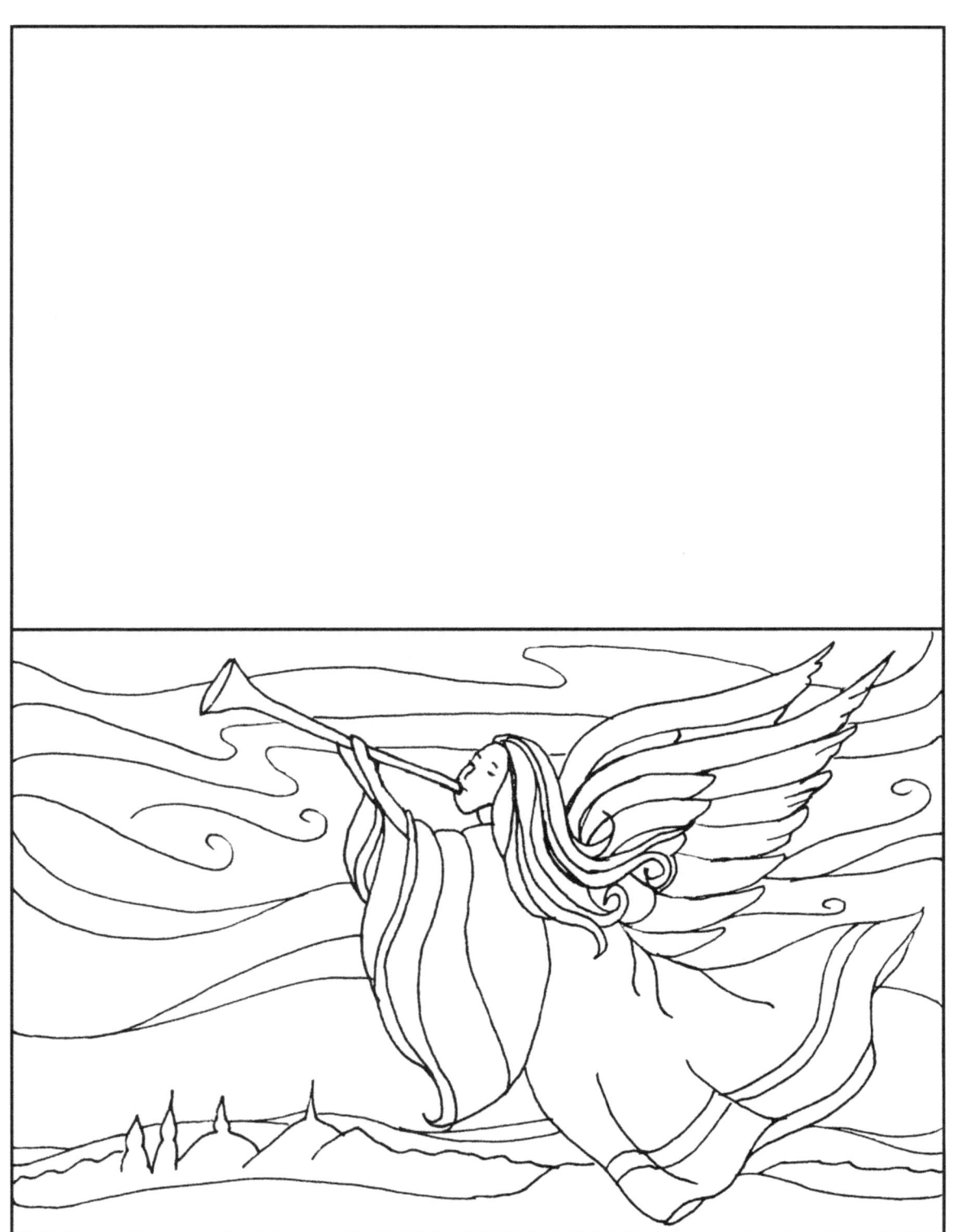

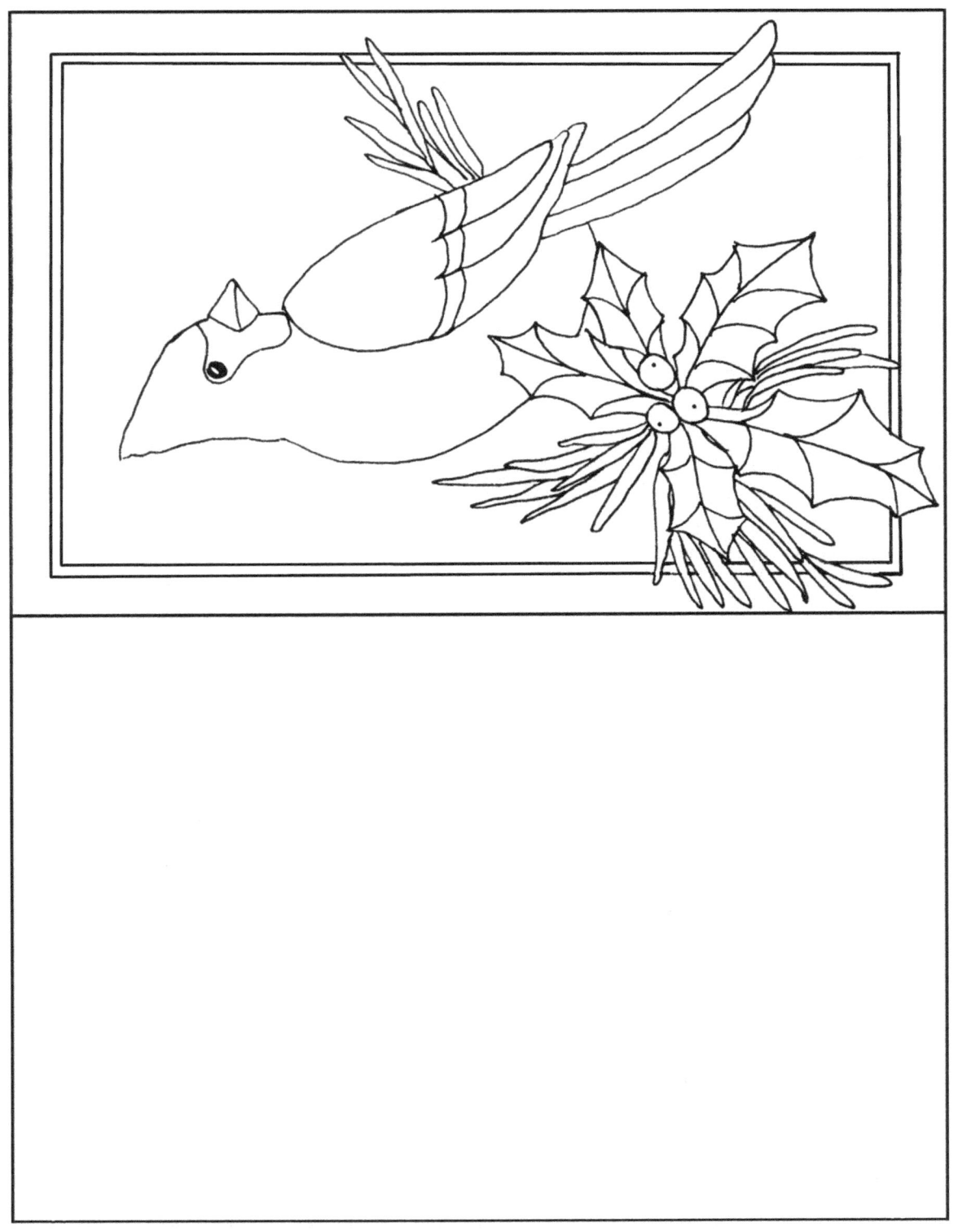

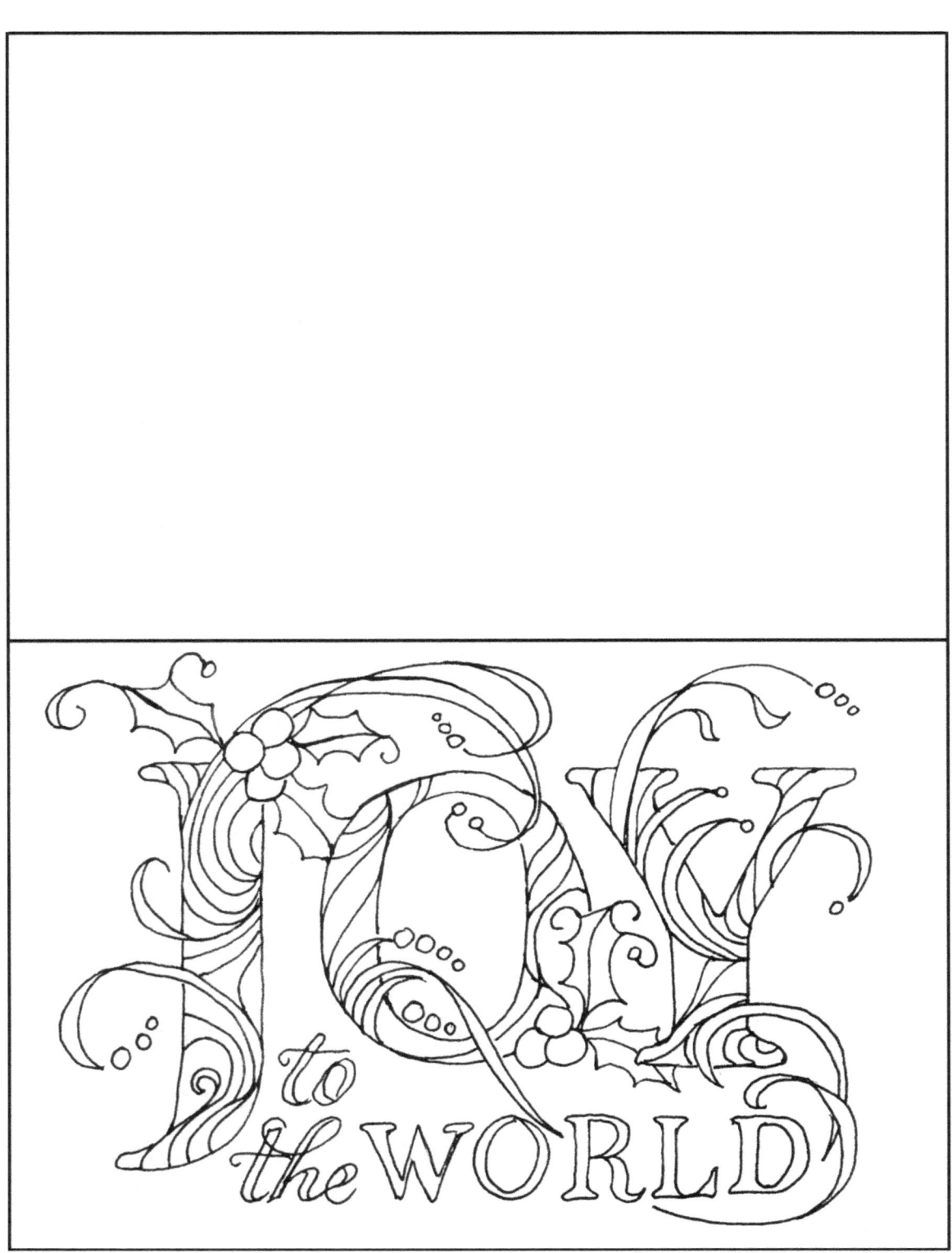

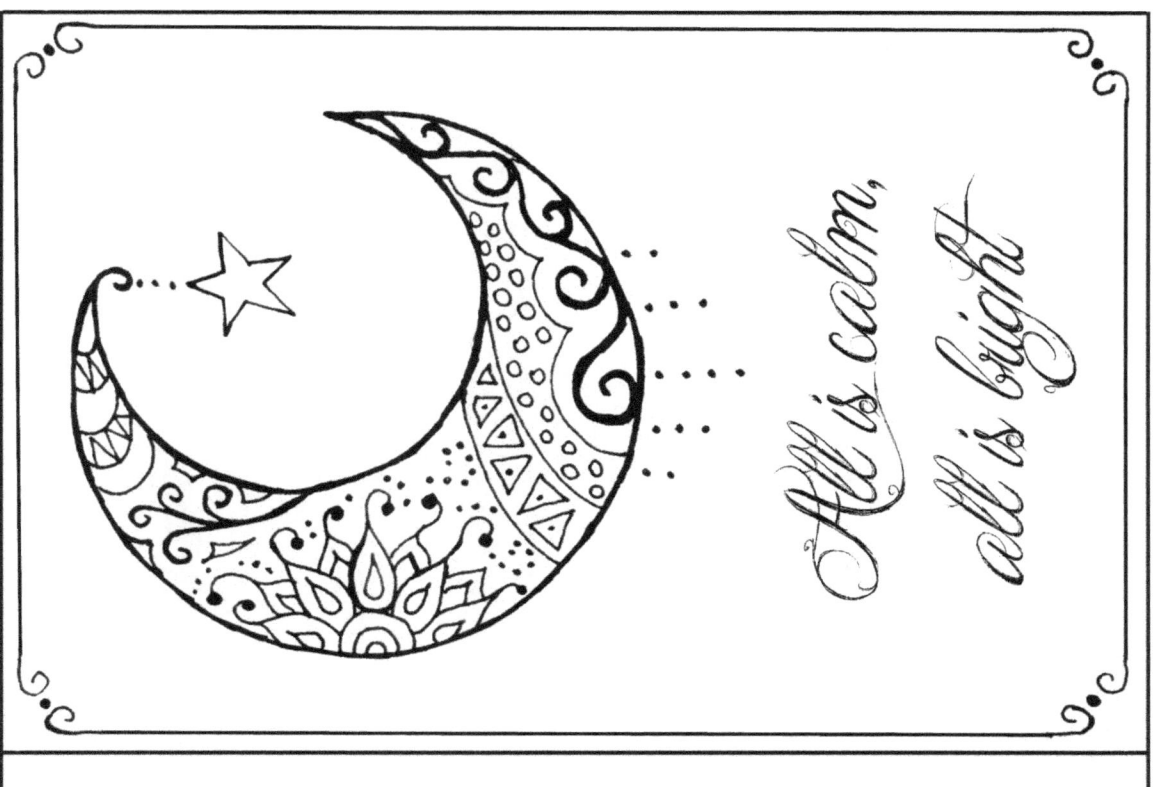

All is calm, all is bright

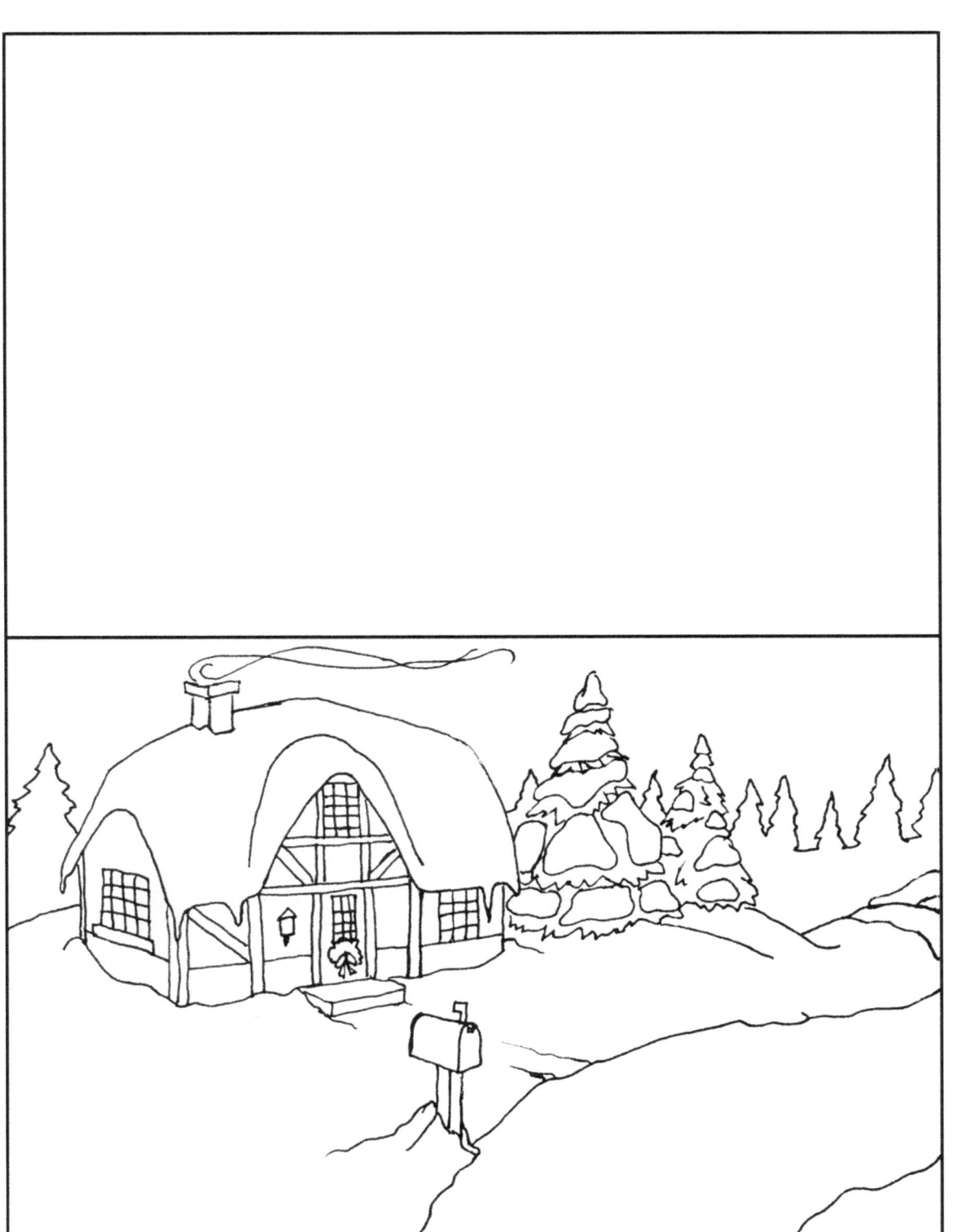

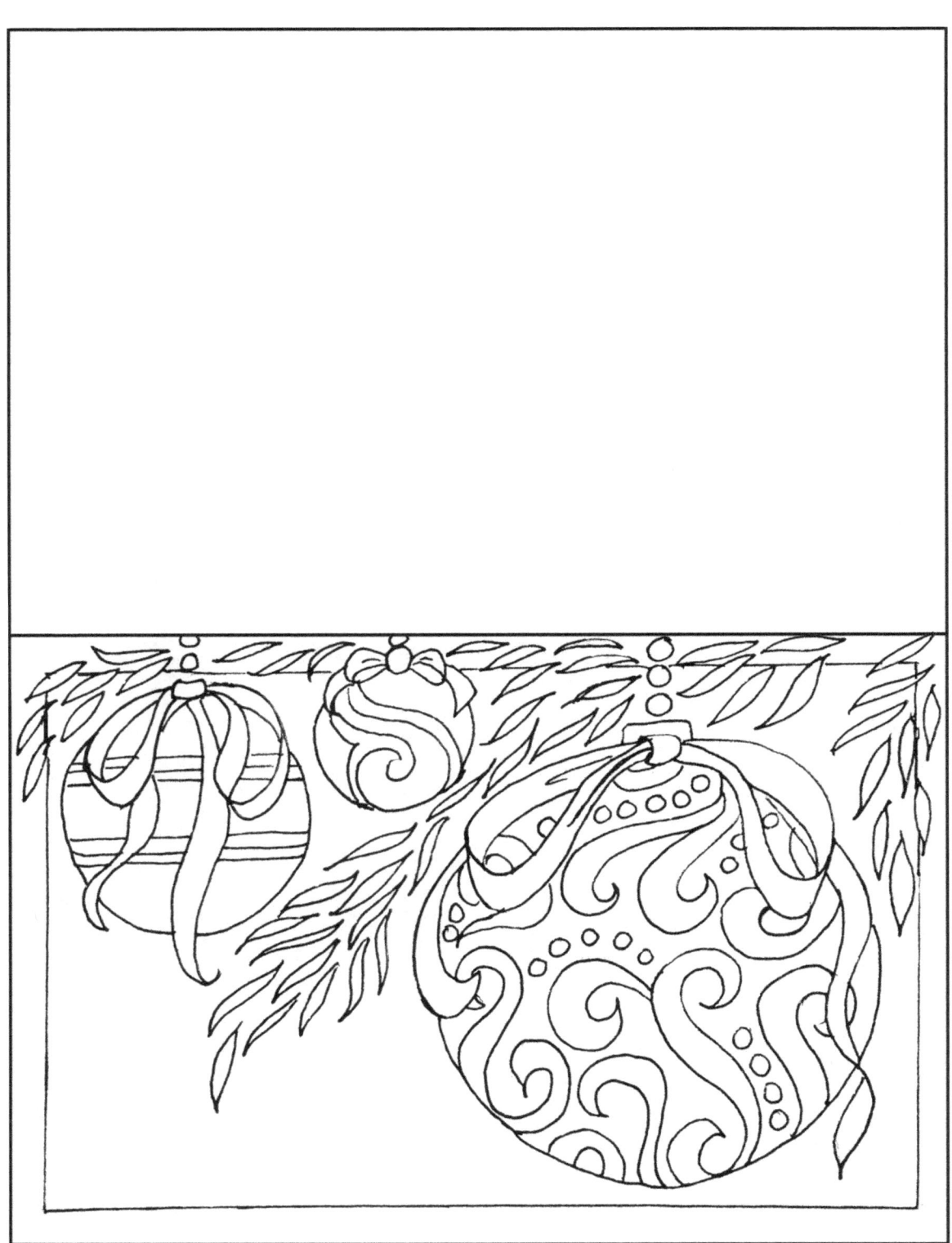

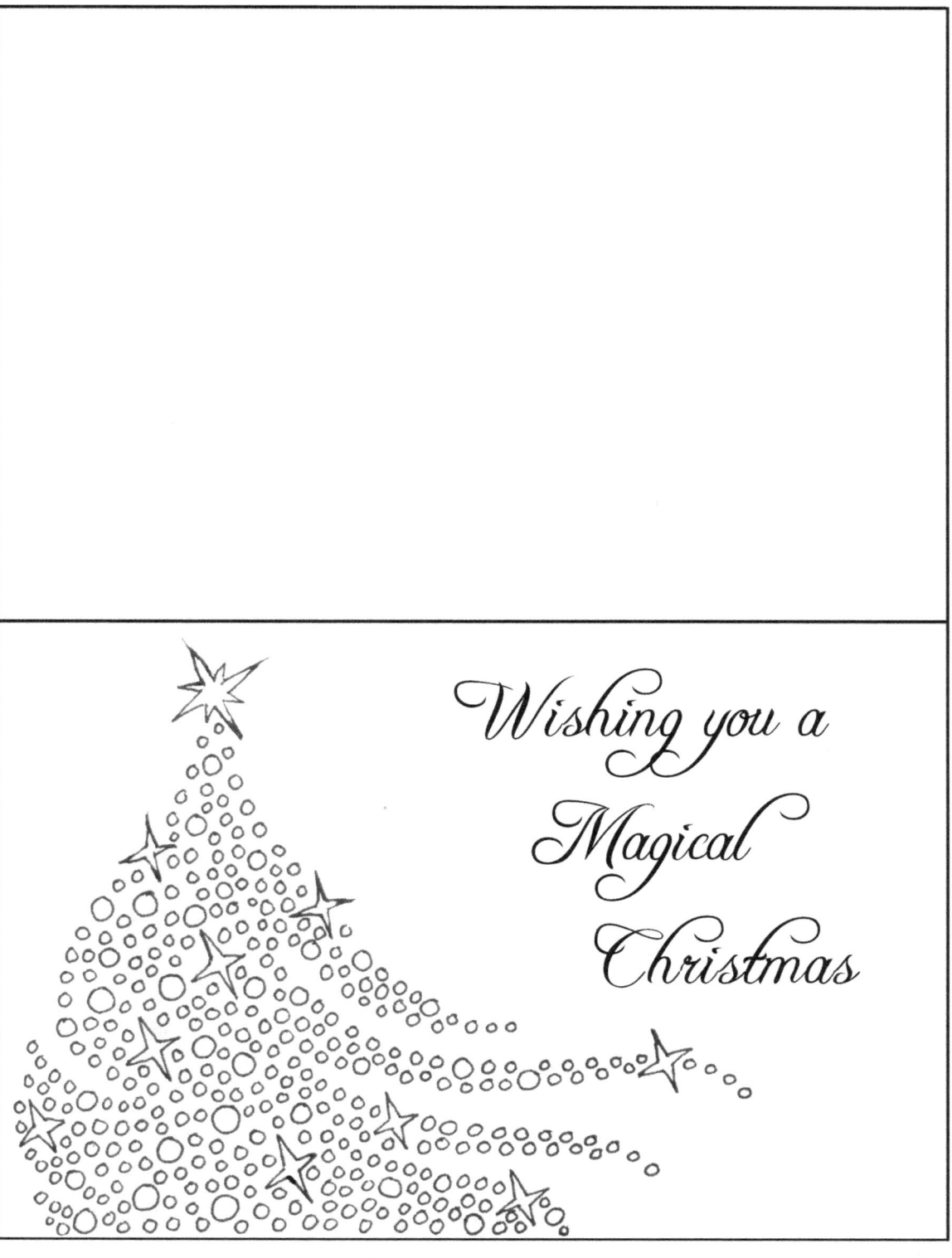

Wishing you a
Magical
Christmas

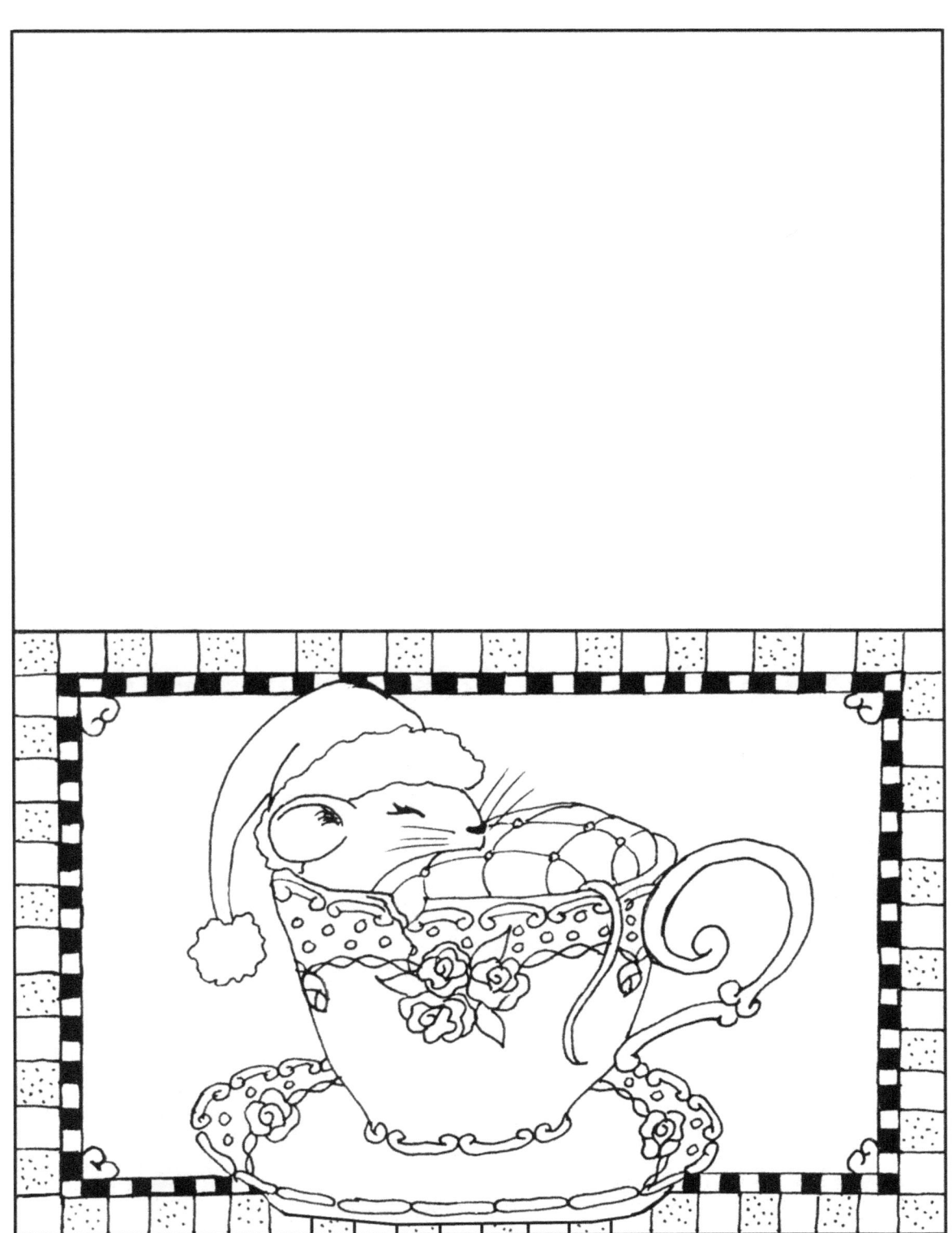

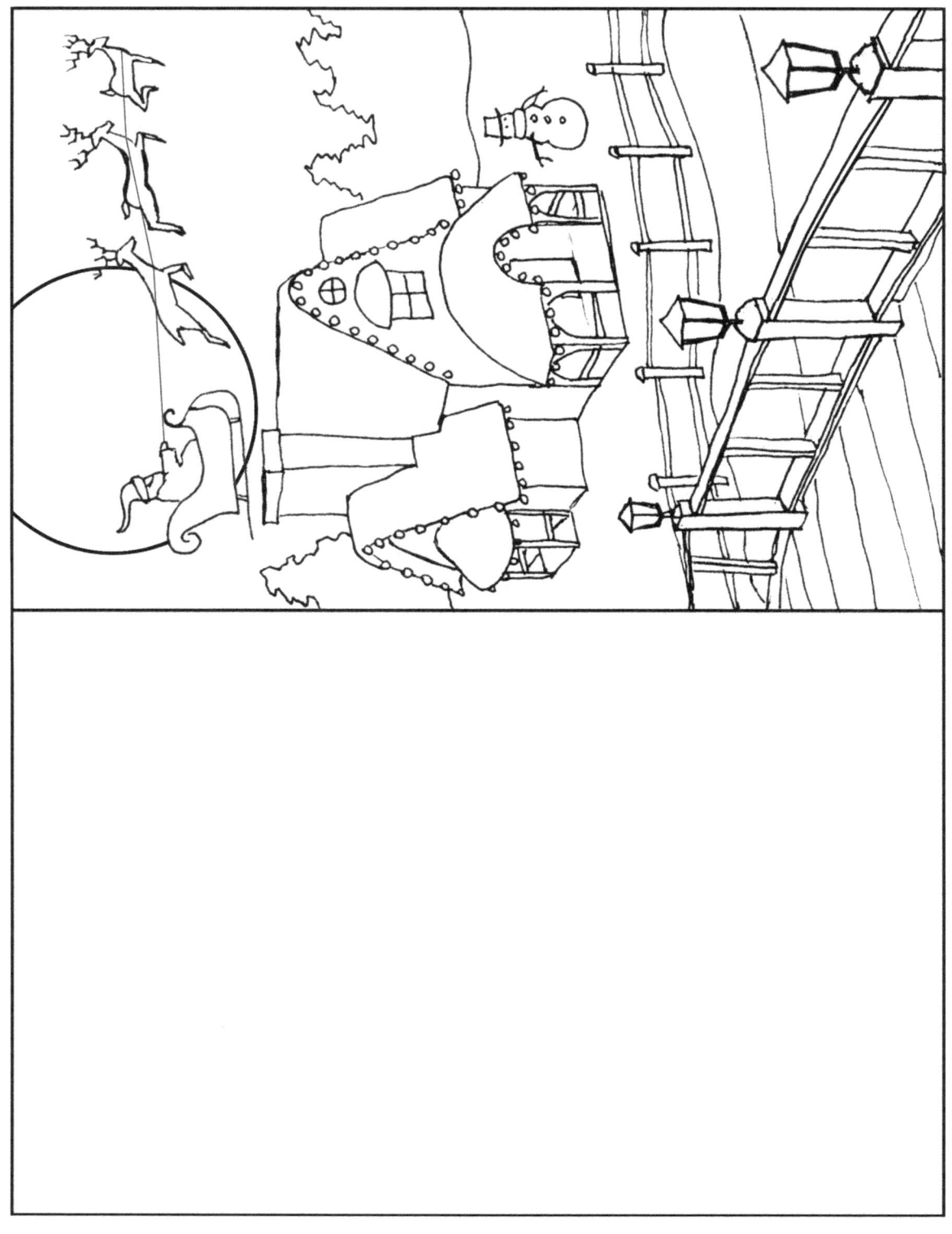

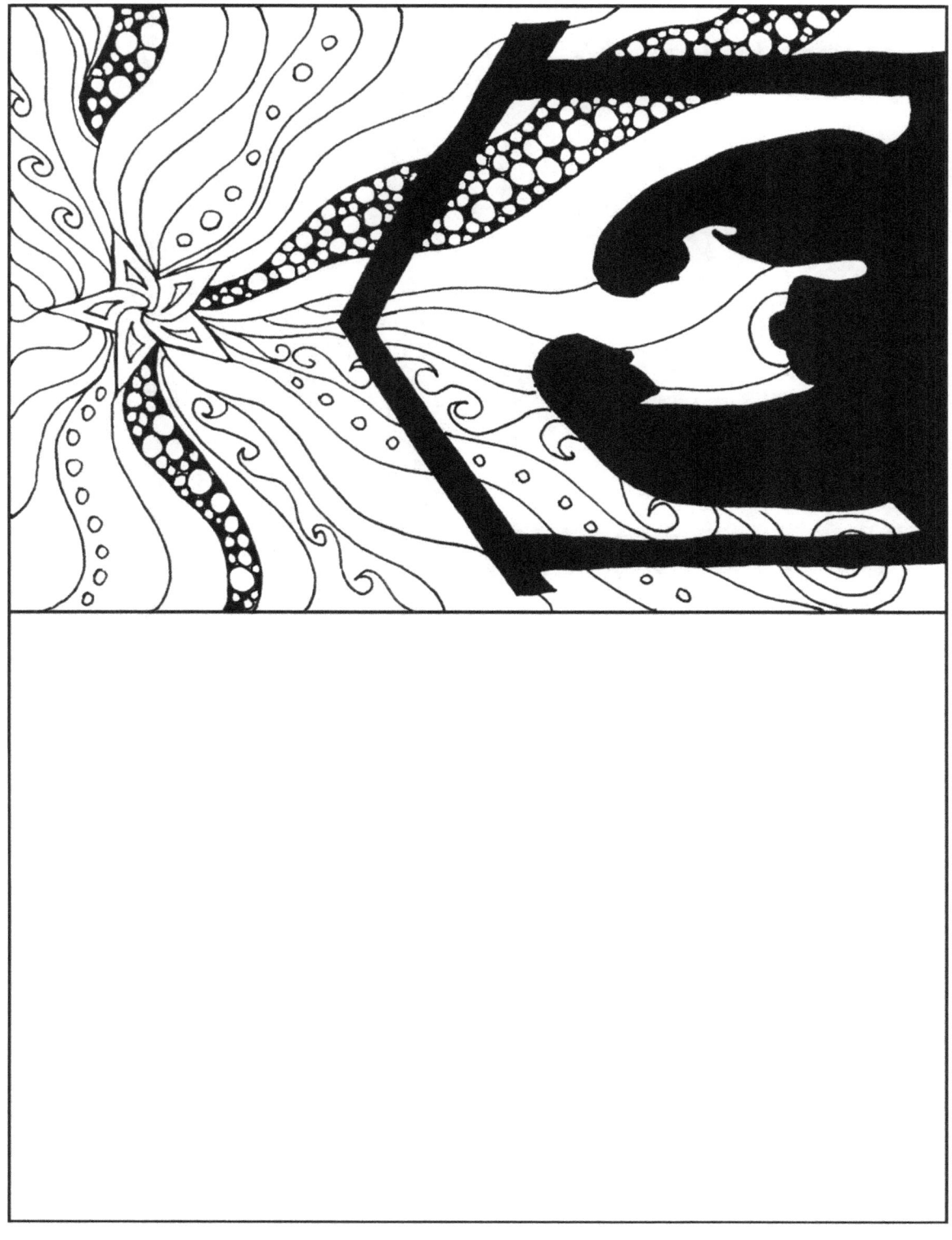

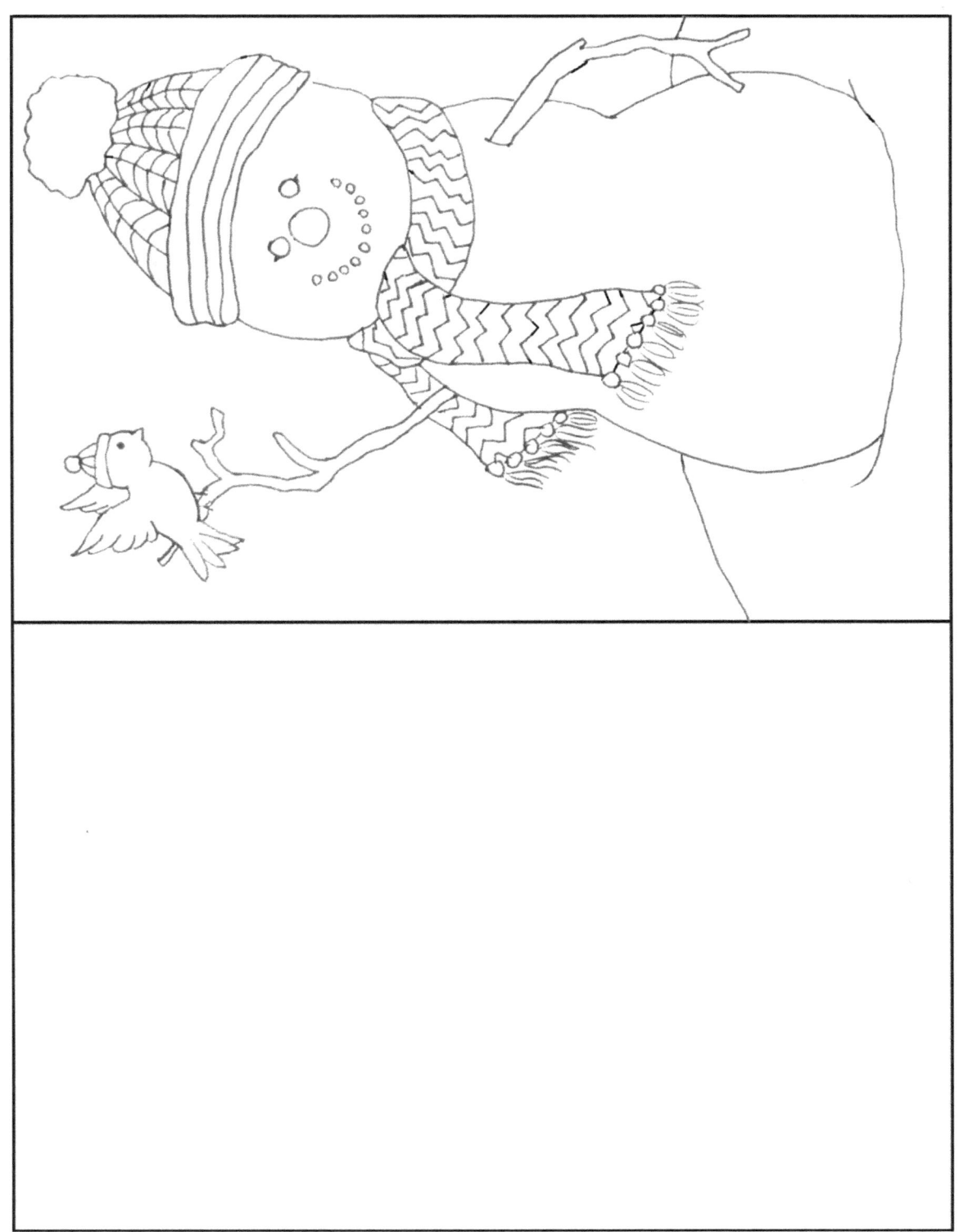

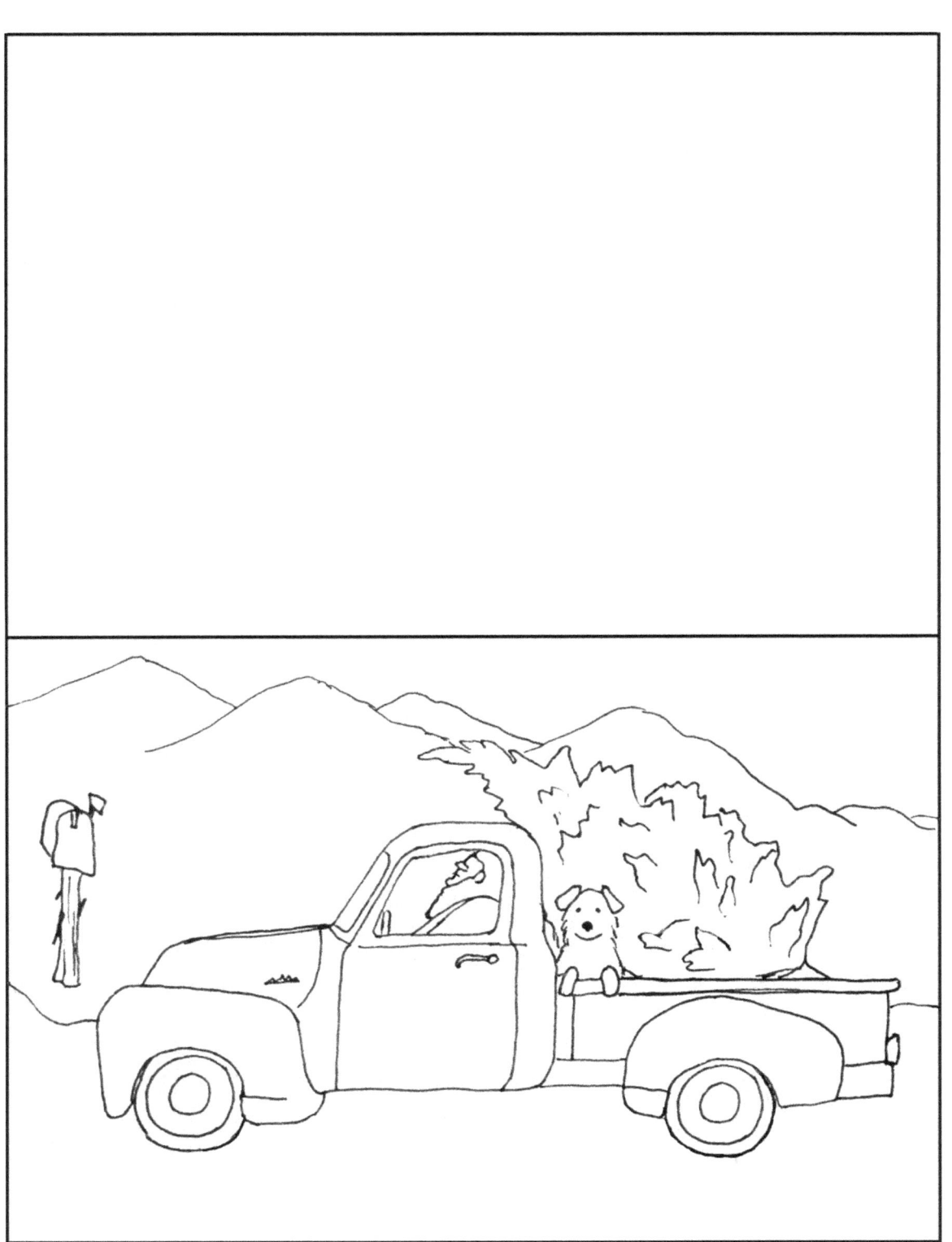

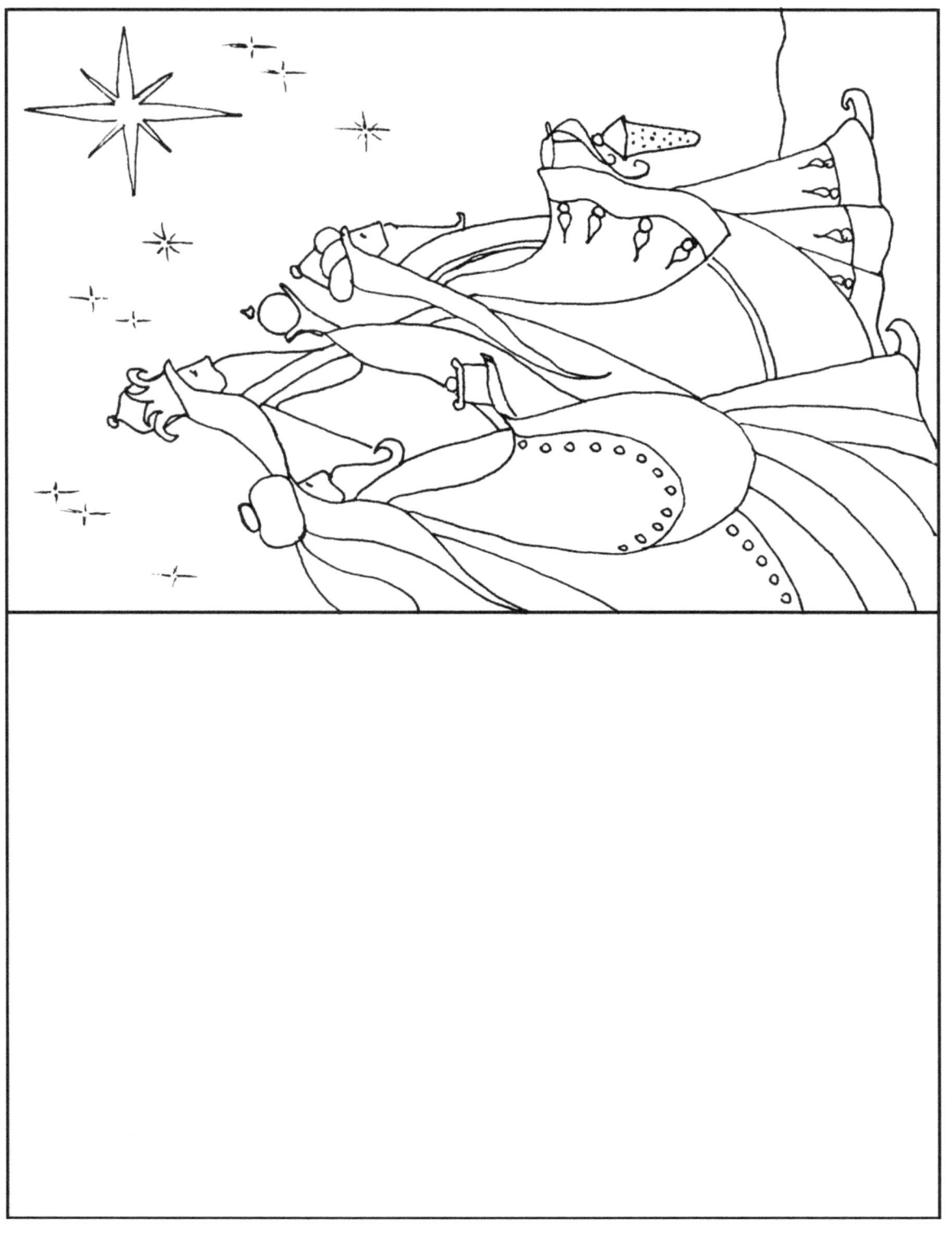

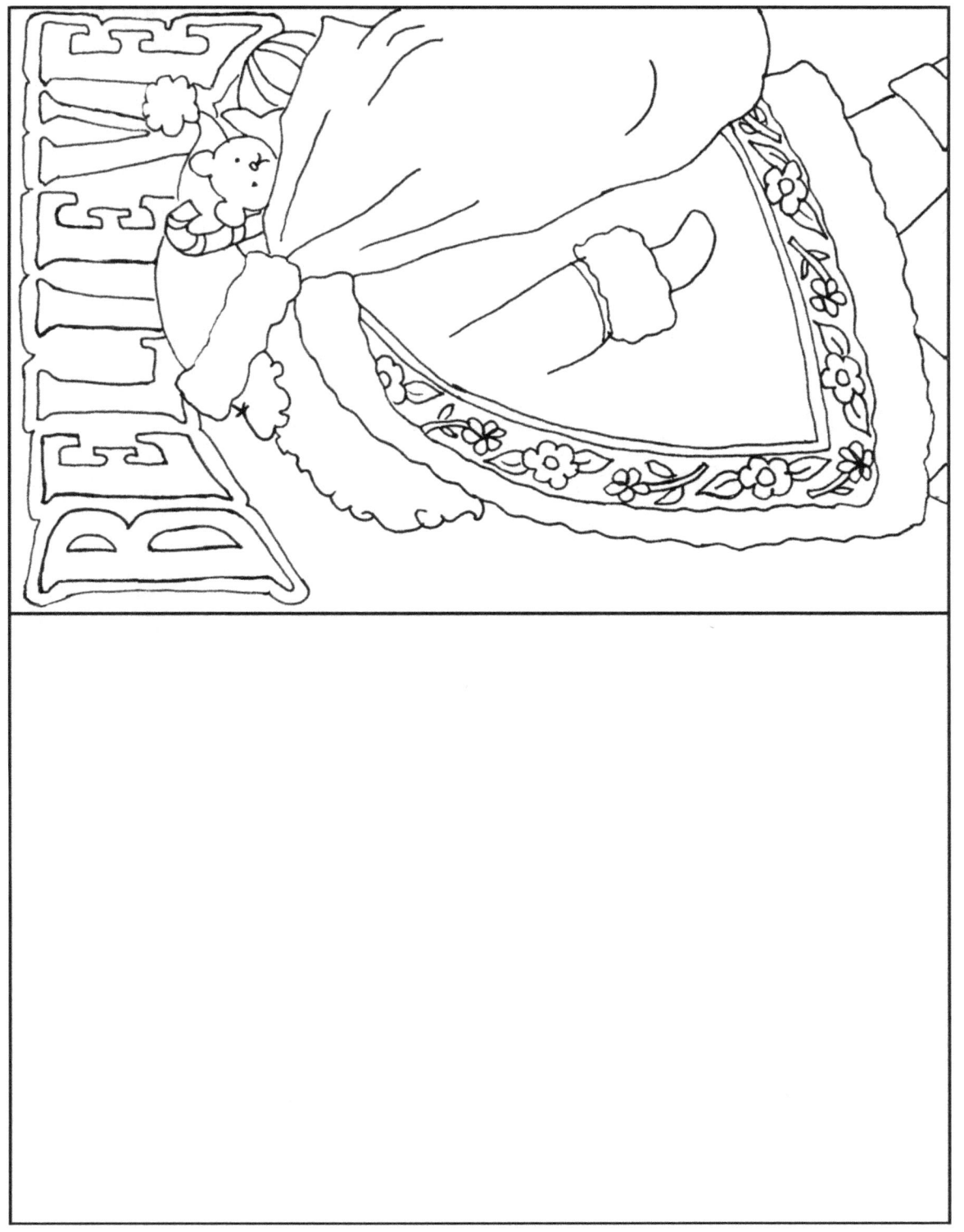

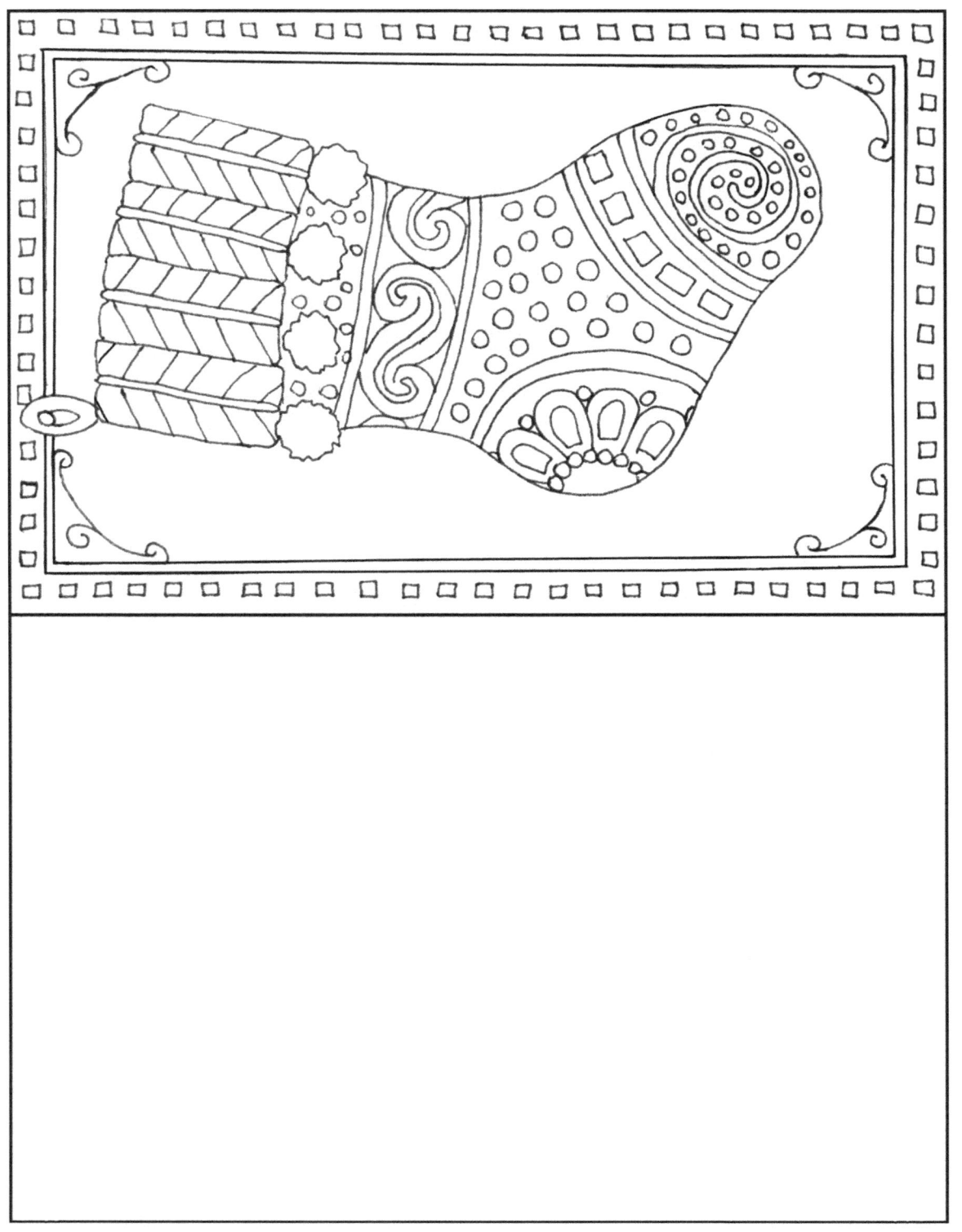

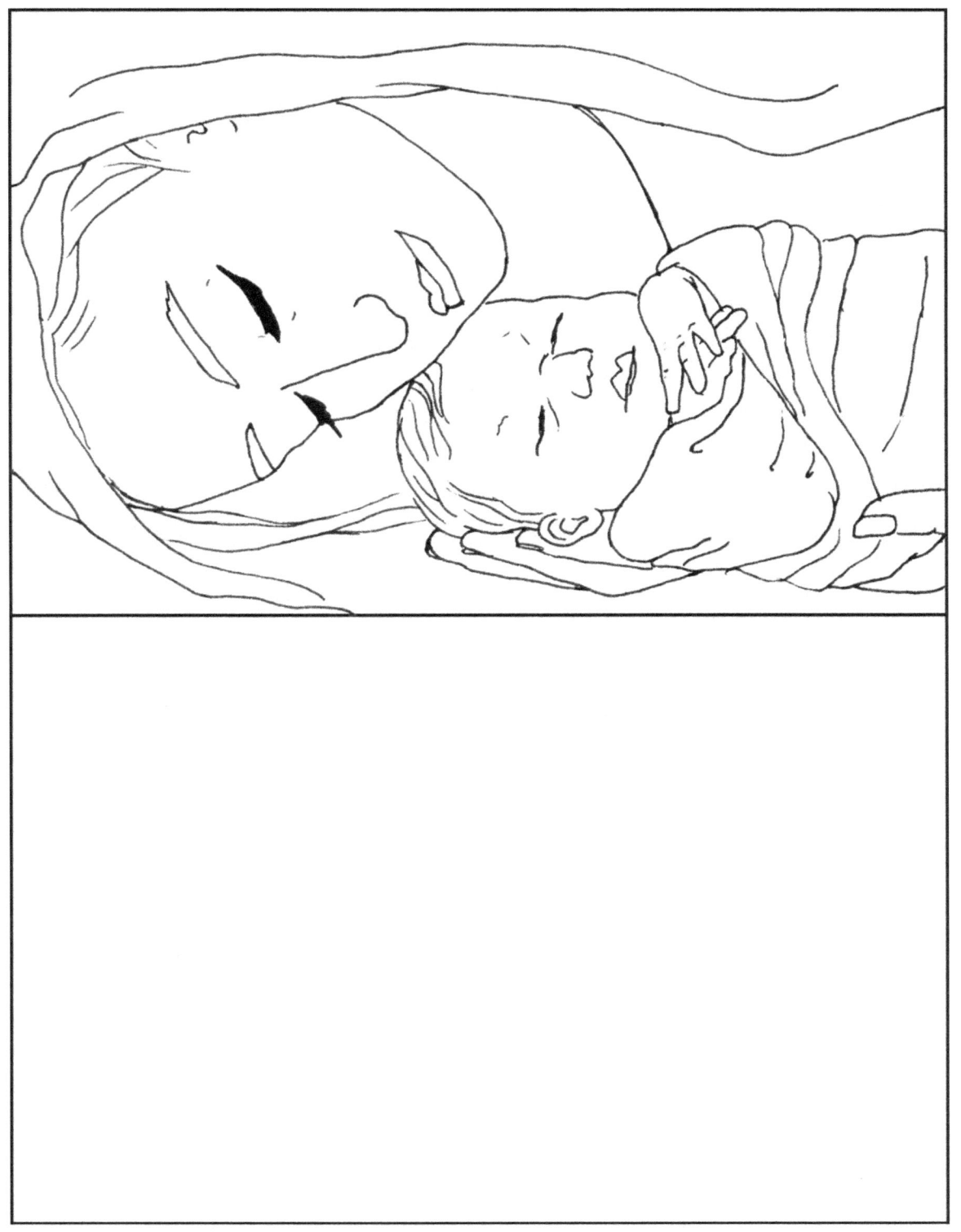

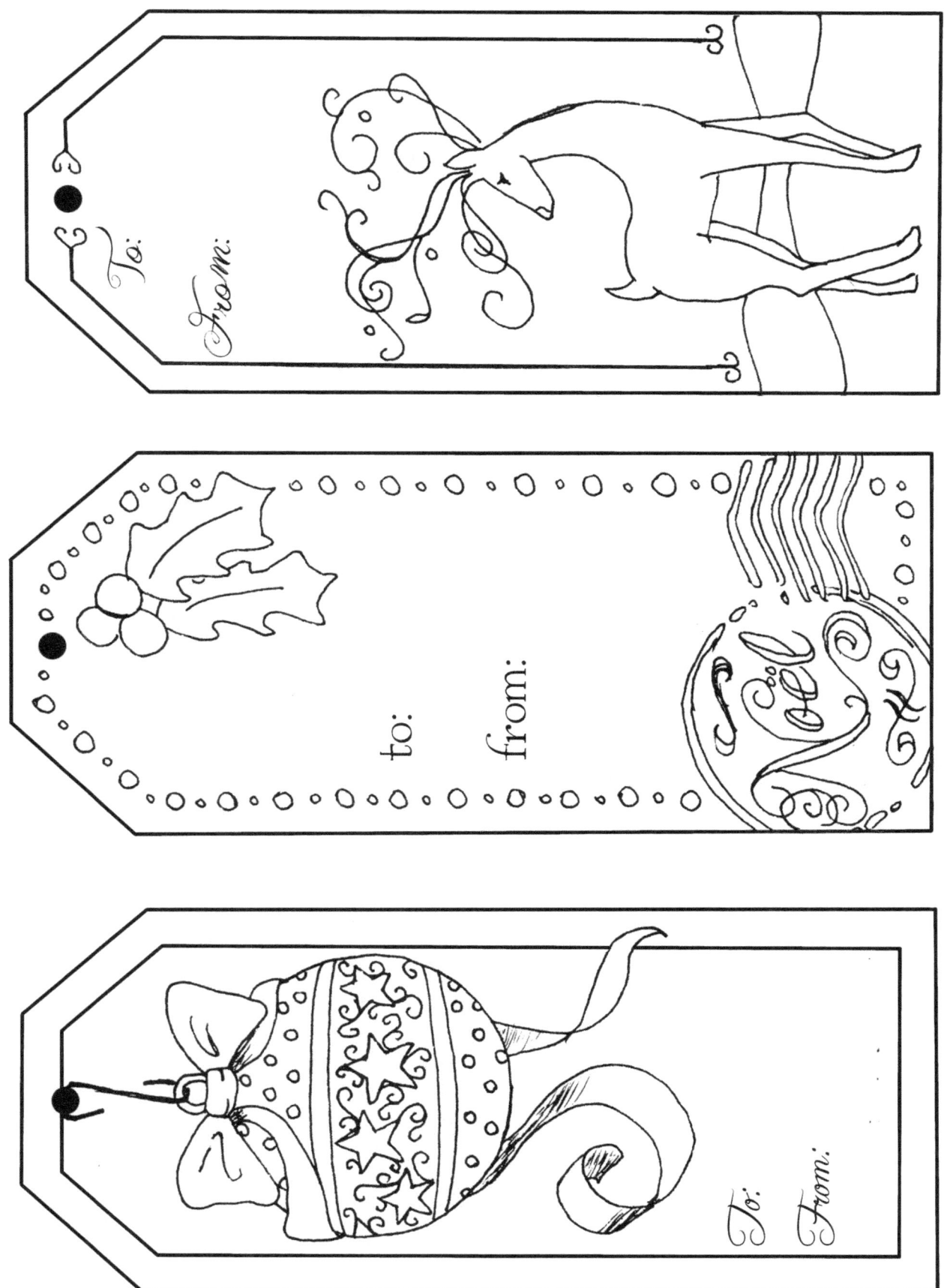

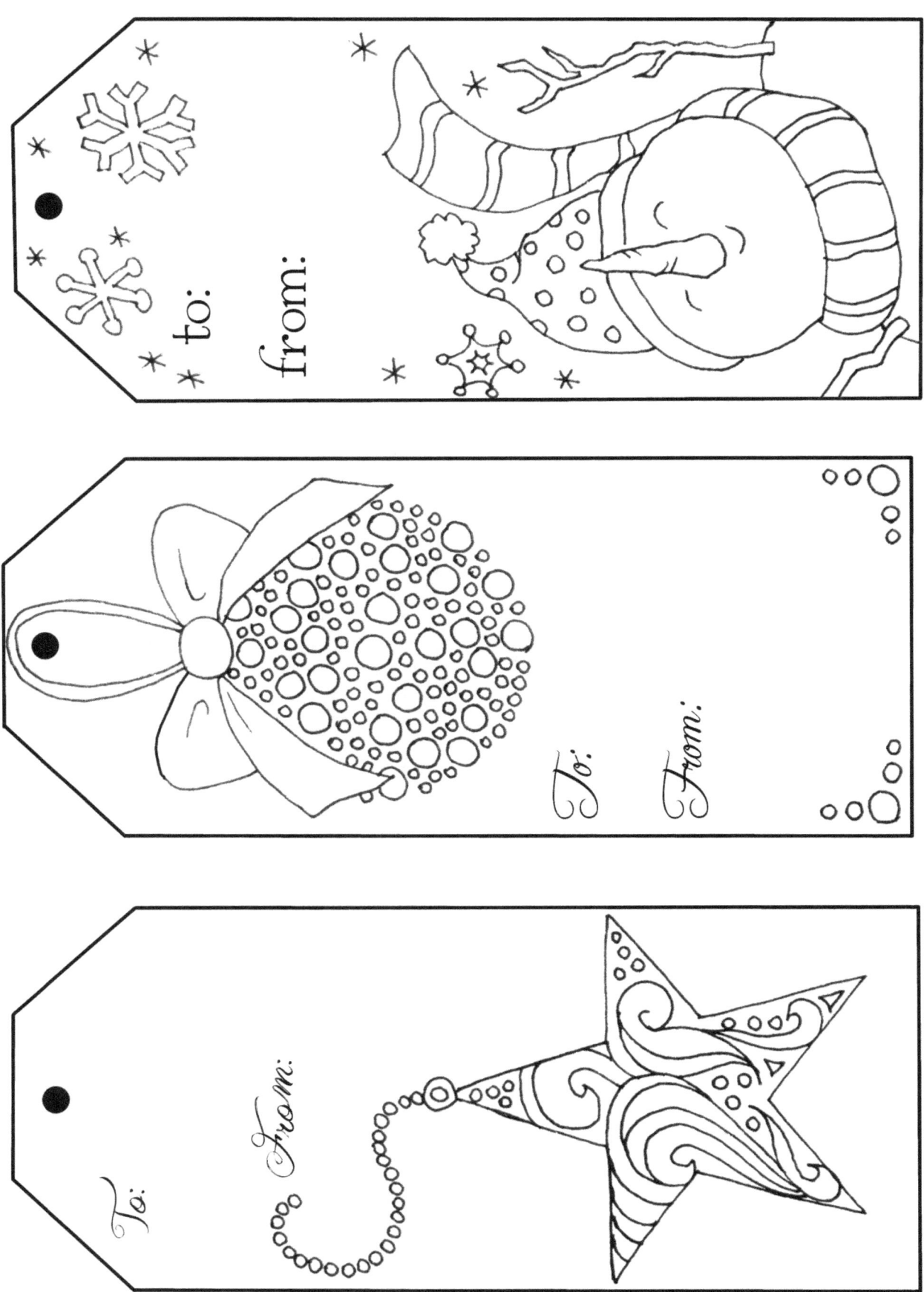

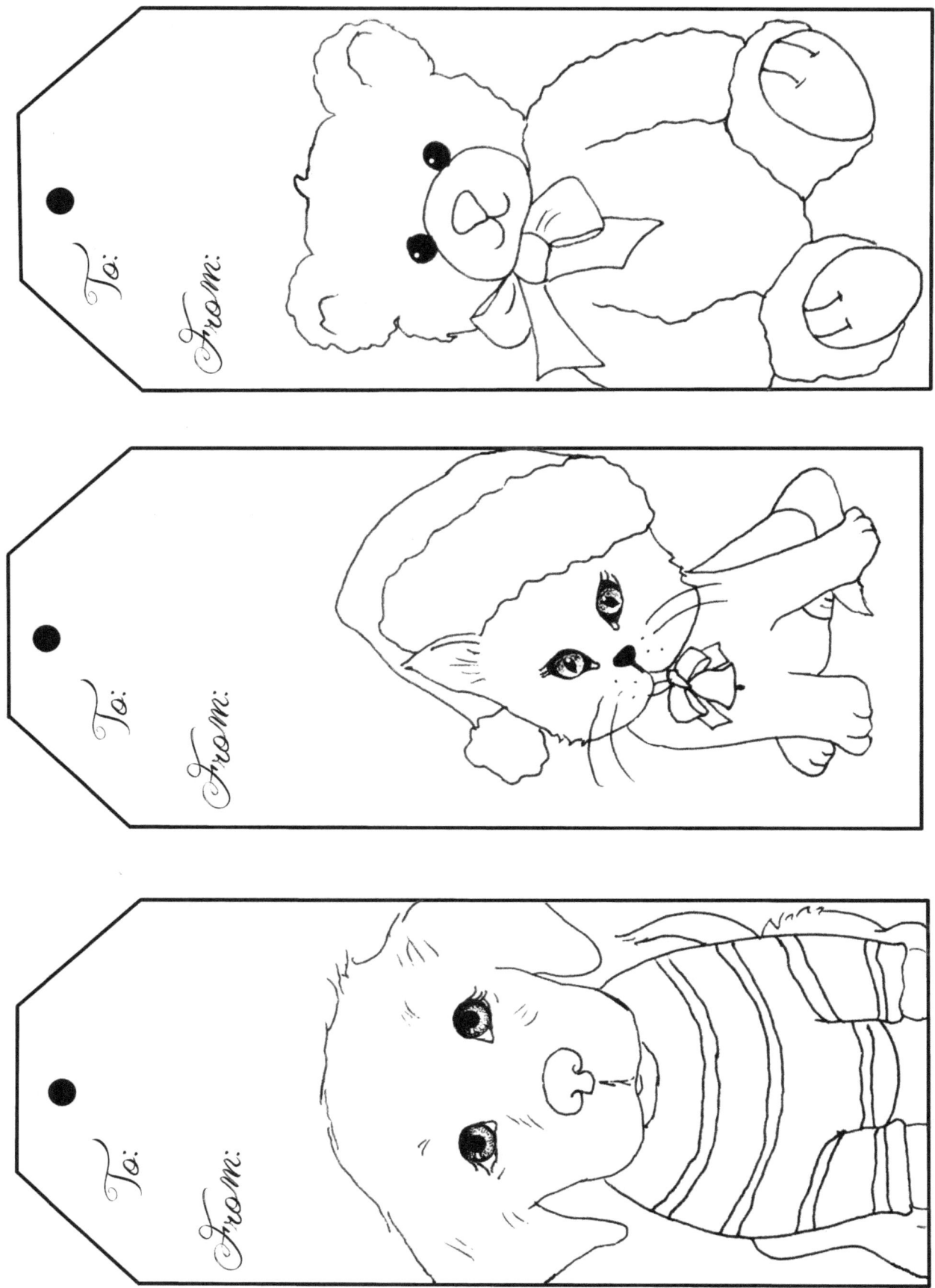

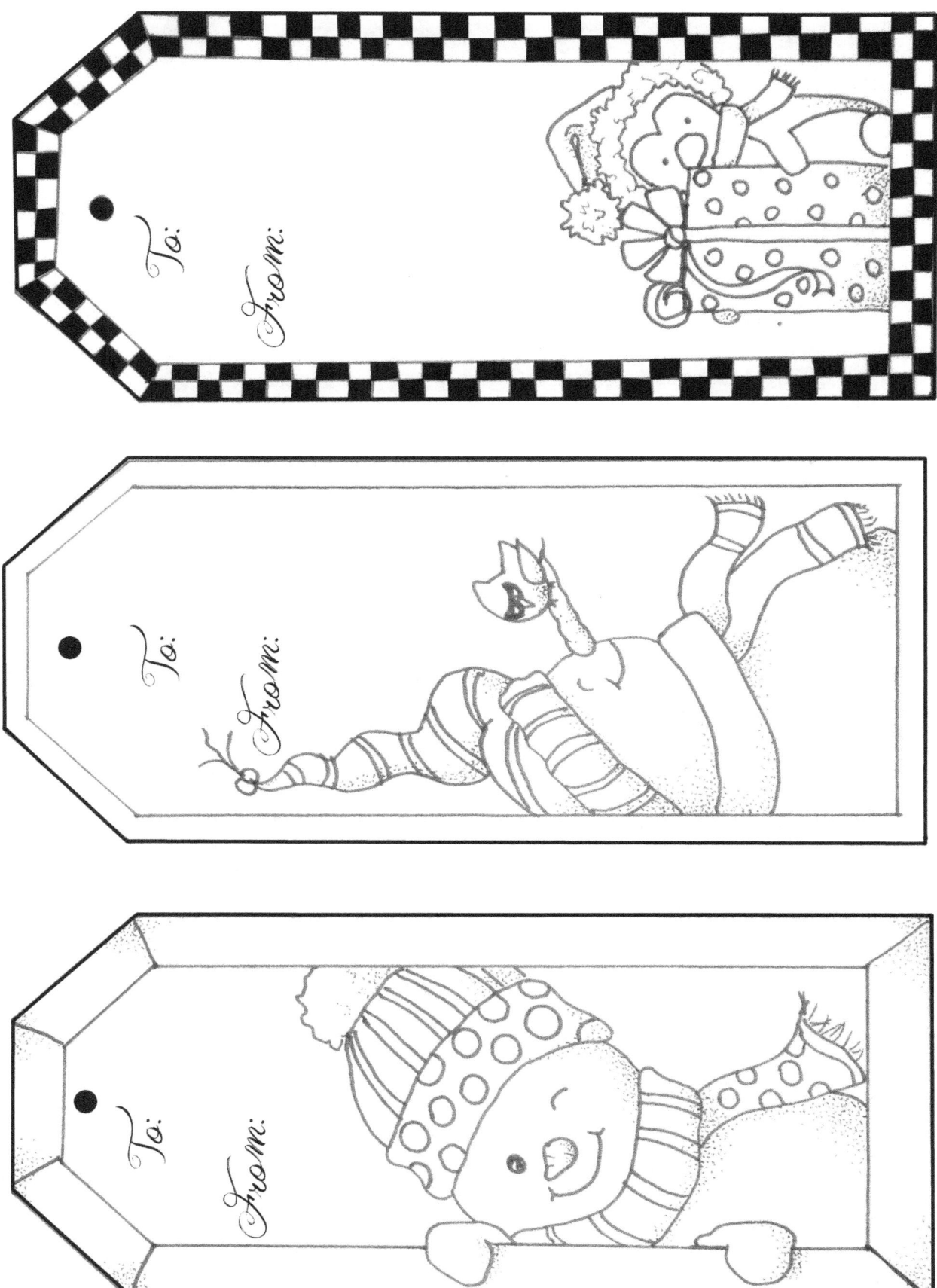

To: From:

To: From:

To: From:

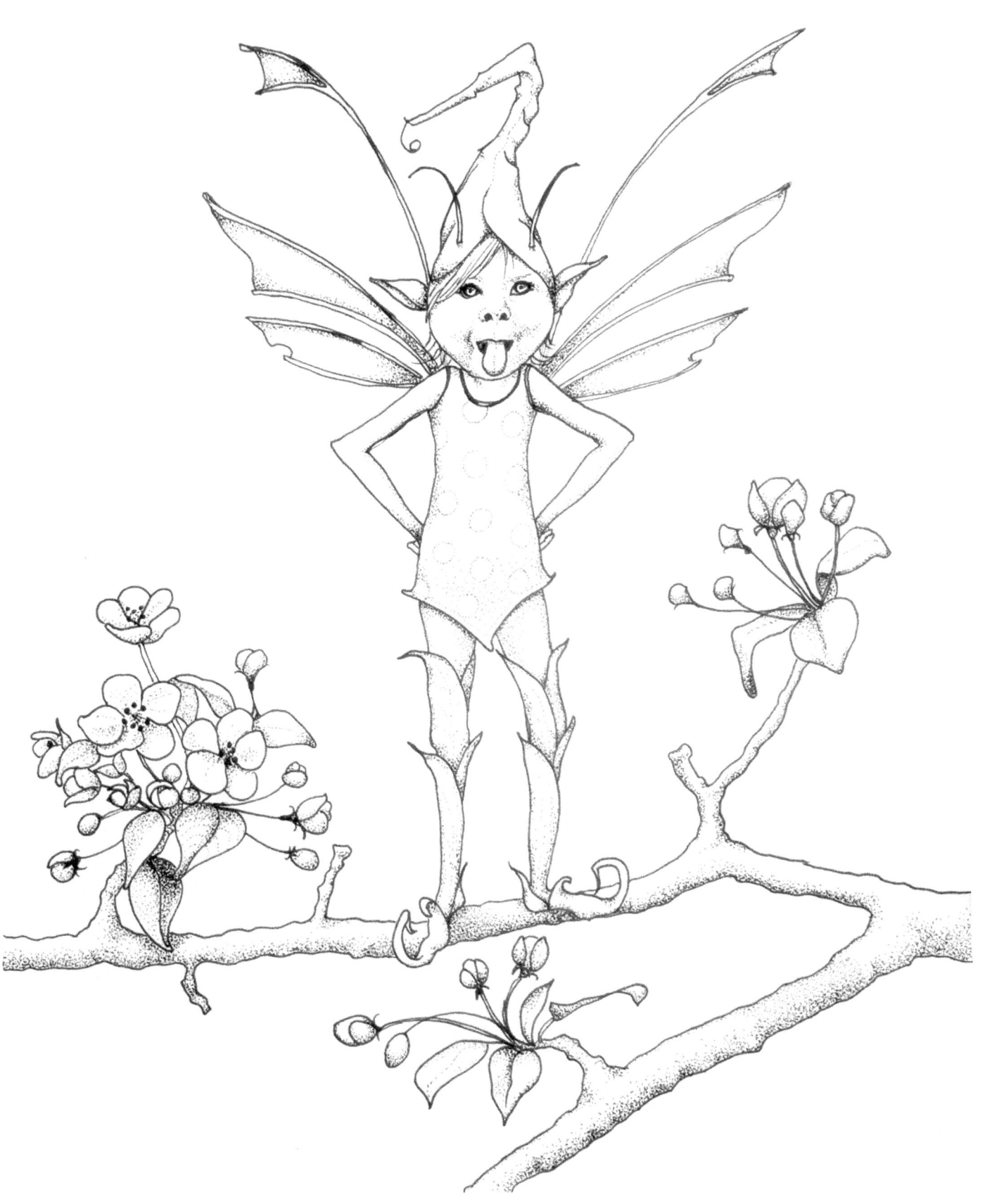

BONUS PAGE from Dragonfly Dreams & Fairy Wings by Cheryl Casey

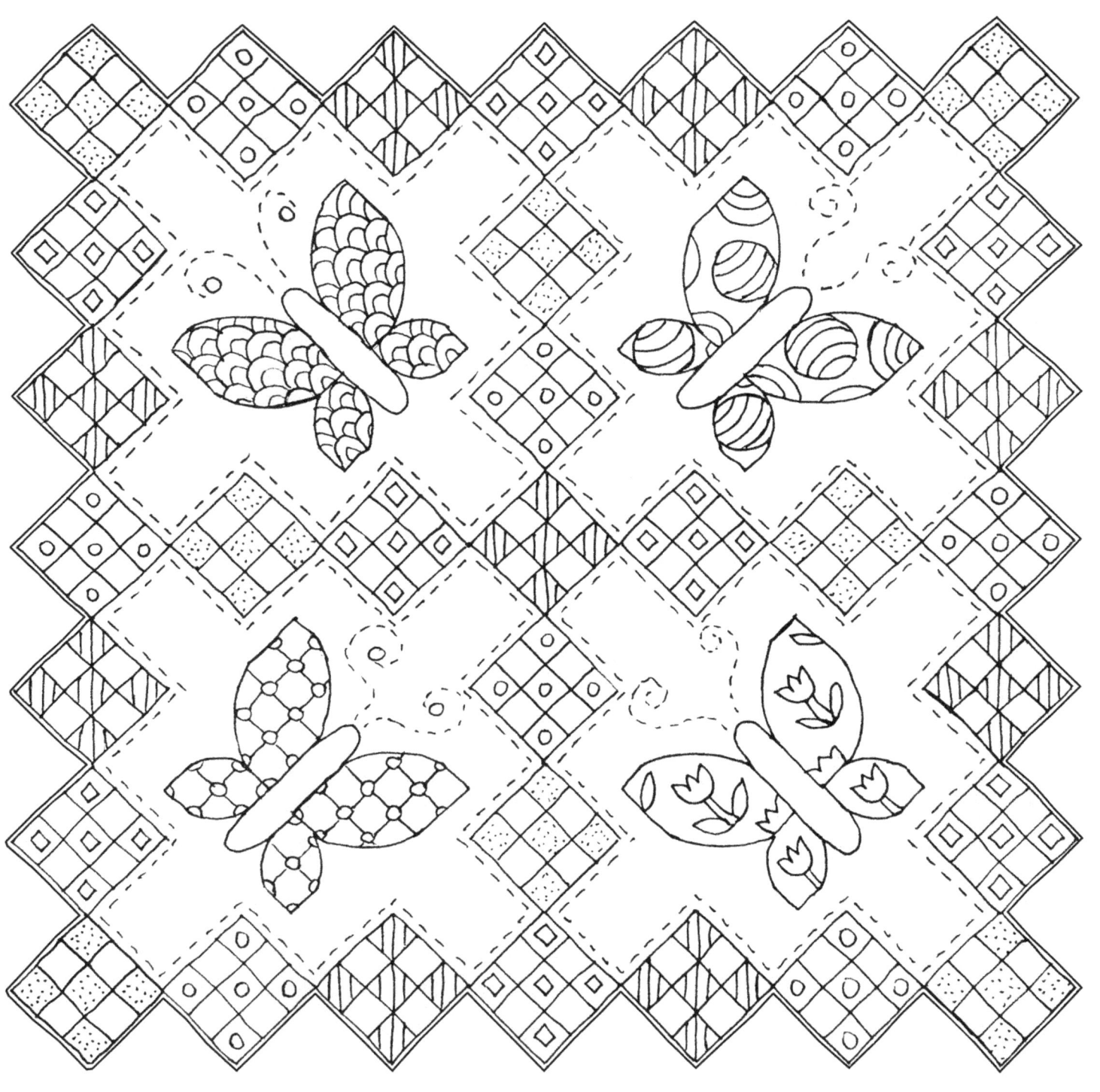

BONUS PAGE from Grandma's Quilts by Cheryl Casey

www.ingramcontent.com/pod-product-compliance
Lightning Source LLC
Chambersburg PA
CBHW080613180526
45168CB00007B/2896